Upon Foreign Soil

John F. Deane

Icarus 3

Upon Foreign Soil

John F. Deane

DEDALUS

Dublin 1999

The Dedalus Press
24 The Heath
Cypress Downs
Dublin 6W
Ireland

© 1999 John F. Deane and The Dedalus Press

ISBN 1 901233 50 2

"Icarus" series, number three, first of March 1999
Edition limited to 500 copies

Dedalus Books are represented and distributed in the UK and Europe by Central Books Ltd., 99 Wallis Road, London E9 5LN

and in the U.S.A. and Canada by Dufour Editions Ltd., P.O.Box 7, Chester Springs, Pennsylvania 19425.

Printed in Ireland by Colour Books Ltd., Dublin

CONTENTS

In his Image	7
By the Rivers of Babylon	8
Food to all Flesh	9
Who Walk in Innocence	10
Who Dwell in a Parched Land	11
In a Pillar of Cloud	13
The Protestants	15
Against an Impious Nation	17
How can we Sing the Lord's Song upon Foreign Soil?	18
In the Dark Places, in the Deep Shadow	20
My Heart was Soured and I was Cut to the Quick	21
Owl of the Waste Places	22
Our Years Vanish as a Sigh	23
As Wax is Melted before the Fire	25
The Catholics	26
The Lord's Song	28
In Splendour and Majesty shall you Ride Forth	33
In a Parched Land	35
Our Days are Consumed like Smoke	36
Sing to the Lord a New Song	38
Truth shall Spring out of the Earth	39
His Mother, and his Mother's Sister, Mary, and Mary Magdalene	40
Owl	42
In his Own Image	43

In his Image

He comes against me on the hilly road,
his fawn suit stained and frayed, his knotted tie
so greased it will never now unloose;
easy to praise the scarlet rose-hips' sheen
and berries that are black stars in a green sky,
but I fear the staggering side-fall of his walk,
the hot vermilion of his skittering eyes,
my fear a shrinking fear, roadside hugging,
till he passes with a slurred "soft day, soft day";
he is, they say, his own crucifixion,
to others gentle as an unspoiled child;
yet in the ditches of our country lanes
blood-berries have never been as manifold
as the drops he's shed over the centuries.

By the Rivers of Babylon

Space, this sunbright Autumn day
between rains; a beech hedgerow
ochre-gold and amber and tender-green,
classical in its fetchedness; the holly

rises to a clear sky, its clutch of berries
still and redolent; moments you touch
the equitable pulsing of the earth; mostly
our world is a high stone-studded door

and there is no way through; but through,
God is at home in his and our suffering
and it is we who dawdle, language-lost,
in a far country we call our own;

he is beyond horizons and beyond beyond,
unviable, impossible, but still we stand
on a sunbright Autumn day and breathe
with satisfaction the green word : *home*.

Food to all Flesh

A small row-boat on Keel Lake,
the water sluppering gently as he rowed,
the easy sh — ssshhhh of the reeds

as we drifted in, and all about us
tufts of bog-cotton like white moths,
the breathing heathers, that lift

into the slopes of Slievemore; all else
the silence of islands, and the awe
of small things wonderful : son,

father, on the one keel, the ripples
lazy and the surfaces of things unbroken;
then the prideful swish of his line

fly-fishing, the curved rod graceful,
till suddenly may-fly were everywhere,
small water-coloured shapes like tissue,

sweet as the host to trout and — *by Jove!*
he whispered, old man astounded again
at the frenzy that is in all living.

Who Walk in Innocence

We gathered, in our gansies, our short
corduroy trousers, and took our places
in a score of desks, eager again
to make our small cacophany of learning;

Mrs Kilbane held the pictures up, bird, gate,
and we spelled out the names, making, at times,
immaculate music; we would have words
for everything. How much alike we were,

with our galluses, our socks, starting out
and steaming, the stoney road from the shore
curving away to continents. But they
were teaching us already a foreign language,

veni sancte spiritus, giving us the transcendent
before we could even name our terrors
of the outside, of night, of facing up
to bullies, they were cowing us with

sacraments and sacramentals,
making their child ascetics and sending us
out from the variegated flock
to skulk in marshes like secretive snipe.

Who Dwell in a Parched Land

Fair day, third Friday, the fairground;
father, big man, parleying
amongst big men. The lorry

growled as it climbed into the yard,
the high red nose of the Dodge,
its labouring, its bulging delicacy;

and all the bodies turned, and all the eyes
and someone dropped the slatted sides and someone else —
tall, long-coated, straight —

began to drop insisting words
onto their heads;
at times his fist was lifted high in emphasis

and the big men shifted in unease;
a sparrow came and cheeped down from a roof
but the man's face was a peregrine's face

and the big men shifted in unease;
father muttered about "untruths"
and someone threw something, someone a stone

and father muttered there's no truth
in stones or hatred either.
The sparrow had flown off; the meagre

cattle stood, too dulled to low;
the lorry made off hurriedly, the tailgate
up, and the men shifted again,

eager once more for bargaining and stout.
That, he said, was the noise
of politics, and that

was desiccated foolishness and now
there is a stench
of lies and violence on the island air.

In a Pillar of Cloud

Creation — to incarnation —
to passion; such history
is a diagram of foolishness;
that we conceive of God

making of himself a depressive
maniac? How should it be
that out of his eternal bliss
he scattered the multiple

seeds of our grief?
The crazy turned himself loose
along the island roads;
stood, full centre

and pissed, thinking his art
placed him as one amongst us;
bare-footed always,
what he begged for, without

wording it, was understanding;
and handed any passing child
the coins we gave to salve
our ego-consciousness;

how could he have been so crazy
to reach so far out from his place
he fell and dashed himself
to pieces? The climb back

is fixed between earth and heaven
where we, broken like him,
gullible, then crestfallen, then
gullible again, are nailed, too,

craziness the root, the rough
bark and multiple leaf in us,
foolishness the measure
we are learning to rename love?

The Protestants

July and August they came south, with their
citric accents, their volubility;
we whispered together of orangemen,

B specials, how they tortured Catholics
and battered them down. Around St Thomas's
a mountain mist was visiting; a wren

skittered irreverently through the alders;
we hid our bikes in a fuchsia hedge, bravely
we left the road and pushed the grincing

iron turnstile; a gravel path curved under trees;
we were intruding, they
were the settlers, cleaving to high ground, we

the natives, feckless, scattered along the shores.
Gravestones stood around their church
with bigger crosses, better kept, the names

were colours: olive, violet, black;
we wondered were there any protestant saints;
then, daring the devil, we hoisted one another

to the window ledges to peer within,
and found it true! bare high pews
with cushioned kneelers, without the stations,

but plaques on the walls for lords and soldiers
and no lamp lit before the altar. Now I could relish
our God, cosy, of hobs and lights and

family pictures. But the gate
shrieked at the road and we
panicked!

if we were caught
we would be cursed and flung
into Protestant darkness.

Against an Impious Nation

Remember, he said, always
your patriot dead; remember
bullet-holes in Dublin walls,
how they shot poor Connolly;
you are Gaelic, he said, remember,
with a language more ancient than theirs

and richer in its poetry;
briste, geannsaí, cóta mór;
how they blighted your faith,
your crops and your sainted names.
Everything abominable, he said,
is rooted there : divorce

and arrogance, the Queen, and sex.
But all the Nultys, one by one,
in Autumn set out for Liverpool;
the Glynns had pensions from the Crown;
and all the Christmas cards arrived
from Coventry, Birmingham and Leeds.

How Can We Sing the Lord's Song upon Foreign Soil?

I woke to a fraught and un-
familiar darkness; I sensed
the simperings of a sweet rain,
pre-dawn breezes in the pines;

in my sleep it had begun already,
the creaking of a cart,
the slow-rhythm, dull, hoof-
beats of a plodding farm horse;

I drowsed on in my comfort.
I heard it then outside our gate,
and the urgent, hushed, voices,
nervous shiftings against the dark;

one voice rose a moment
in distress, like a furred animal
transfixed suddenly and I
was awake to the sound of the approaching

bus, its labouring through the gears to a
stop. It stayed. Ticking.
I could imagine the trunk
tied round with fishing-rope,

how it was hoisted up
under tarpaulin on the bus roof;
I imagined the awkward gestures,
embarrassed kisses and knobbled words

that had been offered long before,
how the hurt was held back, the way
you hold your palm to your side
to contain the suffering. The bus

moved, loudly, and shifted quickly
into silence. A while. Then the creaking
of a cart, the same, slow rhythmic plod
of the hoof-beats of the horse.

In the Dark Places, in the Deep Shadow

He held the bike away
lest it snap its fangs against him;

his hair was flat as wet straw,
his face ridged like turned clay,

his hands on the chrome bars brown twigs;
he mounted, warily, as a cowboy in our old films

would mount an unbroken stallion;
a soiled brown coat flapped about a frame

taut as the recalcitrant bike —
his route the longest distance between points;

and then he fell, toppling, bike and all
into the drain, down beyond Lineen's stores.

Afflicted! was the word they used, to be drunk, they said,
is to have sinned mortally against the Lord;

sin, they said, must be despised and shunned
and I imagined his scalding nosedive into Hell.

How glad I was when he rose onto the road
like a Signorelli figure in the resurrection of the dead.

My Heart was Soured
and I was Cut to the Quick

Her hands were flour up to the elbows; dough
like small gobbets of flesh, adhered; soon
her fingers were stained with juice, like blood-flow;
her apron was round towers and a green moon;
she sang the patriotic songs: *God save
Ireland*, and *A Nation once again* . . .
Then there was Pearse, and mothers, how they gave
their sons in sacrifice; if I had been
older I'd not have paid attention, but a green
bitterness spread in me, angers glowed
and knotted together in my mind; she would insist
that we were scions of O'Malley, pirate queen.
When my knife cut, an orchard richness flowed —
blackberries and tart apples blent beneath the crust.

Owl of the Waste Places

All of us sitting quietly, he
pacing the kitchen floor, pacing,
head bowed and pacing
outside the glow of the lamp;

we, hunched, not frightened,
the security of our living
taut and humming, like a
rubber band; till I knew

we are all broken, carrying
our weight of distress and frustrated
longing, pacing, as if by
friction of our bodies against

the world's air we may yet
for however little a space,
outside the glow of the lamp
achieve a small balance.

Our Years Vanish as a Sigh

She was doing the crossword;
there was a small tea-stain
like dried blood on the table cloth;

ageing, but not old,
the words escaping her, across
and down . . .

He stood awhile above her;
faith in our own mortality
the most difficult of all.

He spoke, circling her,
offering clues, but could not
say the word; behind it

was their love,
lifetimes together;
ahead of it . . .

Anyway she would refuse
to hear. He softened it. The lungs,
a scarring, cigarettes . . .

She glanced up a moment, shadows
passing on her face like clouds
across a meadow. Looked

down again. A word, she said,
six letters, beginning C,
to mean *assent* . . .

As Wax is Melted before the Fire

Should you shift attention from me
for the moment of a moment, I must
disappear at once into nothingness;
I try to love you, the way the centipede,
the way the cat, loves you, its diamond teeth
fastened in a blackbird's flesh, the way the bird
loves you, its song, its ripped-out throat;
everything that stands stands in your sustaining love :
the scorpion, the rat, the poison snake,
Paisley, Hussein, Milosevic,
leach and slug and wasp and clegg,
Thatcher, Reagan, Pinochet —
all of us, like snails, endeavouring to haul
our burdens and defences down the motorway.

The Catholics

Outside the church the felons slouched,
fag-butts fisted, eyes
mocking and watchful; we, the stolid

Roman citizens, affected to despise them;
but I was envious,
that nonchalance, the daring;

outside the church sheep dithered,
it was acceptable to hobble them,
to break dull sticks on a donkey's rump,

to crack a sheep-dog's leg with viciousness;
outside the church
were drunks, depressives, and the mad

in old cottages down long and fuchsia-crowded lanes;
dancehalls,
the desultory gropings for white flesh,

while snipe were arrows across the dark
and curlews in the distance pricked out loneliness;
I envied those that walked in darkness.

In their own time they entered, offering
scandal, the sign of the cross a quick
brushing of cobwebs from the face.

Who was their God? the good God
of flesh and ploshy places, of hands
red from clods and fish-scales, that foolish

adequate God whose perfecting hands
created all unequal.
But sometimes in the church

morning light brought flights of angels to the walls
passing from the bright, delectable world outside
to where we worshipped.

The Lord's Song

The world and its machinations happened
somewhere off the coast : ships
passing across a far horizon,
confusion of lights and a dark
smoke heavy on the air.

Achill Island : eagle, wood; all
absence, the golden eagle dead
and the oak roots
awkwardnesses in turf bogs;
except for acquisitive tourists, absence
is our being, our migrant shifts,
our turgid leanings towards another world,
imaginination filling up the emptiness,
setting tasks, supplying consolations.

This is our hero : Tadhg; his song;
delivered himself hurriedly to the world;
before his mother, milking,
could settle herself,
he fell to earth in the cowhouse
onto soiled straw; you would think
he had some grandiose mission to fulfill,
that his, at least, would be a life of grace.

History happened elsewhere, ours
a theoretical knowledge gleaned
from school-books and adult mutterings,
but we knew the history
of the obedience of the universe to God
and how pain and joy
are the chroniclers of every day.
Our Tadhg lived, on his island,
as if he were the hub of the world.

Ours a small boat culture, lumbering
half-deckers, curraghs, exposing us
to the violent Atlantic. Tadhg
trawled at times, when the weather
permitted; otherwise
he had a few scared sheep
chewing the high sides of the mountain,
a few lean and grudging cattle,
sheep-dogs, cross-eyed, obedient.

Our history is inward, in the silence,
the static
of our struggles and compulsions;
perhaps it was innocence to believe
he was given all the answers
before ever he learned the questions;

growing, the pores begin to widen,
dark urgings filter out of air
into a bleakening soul; a history
hidden, turf smoke and mould and hayrick,
and how the winter sea
alters unalterable shorelines.

No quinqueremes, no armadas
enter the small ports, our spirits
toss on a sea of resignation, our wars
are with hunger, emptiness and pain.

Sometimes, in storms, we live
in the soup of original chaos;
could we call such suffering
redemptive? certainly
it has reduced us, to kindness
and an understanding sympathy;

more often though, in the secret soul,
we are raw with impossible longings, imagination
inventing the cruellest dreams
to torment us; our chronicles
are of baptisms and whist drives,
of the dole and desperate weathers.

Tadhg's was involuntary craziness,
not like the God's
who emptied himself of his divinity
to be a shivering baby in a stench-filled stall
and proceded to a life of foolishness;
if a man may be reduced to nothing
that crazy God may take to him
as the very image of the Godhead.

We have seen old women
rocking themselves in sorrow,
old men worn thin as blackened kelp
from the frictions of work and pain,
and no one counts for anything —
man nor angel — before the destroying sea;
we sigh, and suffer, and sigh again,
to justify our guilt that we are not God.

We have fasted, prayed and suffered,
repented, sinned, repented,
and yet, in our bones, see, and in our eyes
we mock the possibility that there is life
anywhere beyond the heavens.
Can you imagine our shoreman, Tadhg,
stalking heaven with Adonis body?

His, too, a life of sanctity,
reduction of the ego to the crude
necessities of living, and yet
with a warm rheum in the eye,
a willingness to share should anyone
request the sharing; no more
did Peter suffer, nor that Simon
perched as a scald crow on his pile,
nor Anthony in his desert
eyeing the bone-bed of the soul, nor Paul
suffering the twisting thorn in his flesh.

He lay, we saw him, on his batchelor bed,
in the lower room of his batchelor house,
his stagnant body drivelling into death;
we saw the oils delivered, the chrism,
there was a white wax candle,
the murmuring of prayers,
until he breathed more easily and his crumpled face
took on a hint of some beatitude;

he, too, merely a gobbet of flesh
left nailed to the shivering bone;
just one breath more and he is gone
to the far perimeter of his aspirations.

In Splendour and Majesty shall you Ride Forth

We stood, in phalanx, on the driveway;
the wind blew surplices and soutanes,
outlined male limbs, untried, our hands
going uncertainly to our hair;

authority itself was to pass amongst us,
would touch us forever with perfection;
our black shoes gleamed, our spirits shone
from the friction of vows, our soft wills

would be deft reins in his horned hands.
Outriders first, the car like royalty's
purred along the avenue; someone
opened the door for him and he appeared,

smaller than I had expected, stooped
under the weight of greatness, a dangerous
small smile tightening his face, head
lowered but sharp eyes raised and watchful;

voluminous cloths and kingly colours
set him apart and far above but oh!
how we swelled that we, too, were Roman,
this world and the next firmly in our graasp

and the gravelled earth solid beneath our feet.
Leader; manipulative and crafty saint,
unbroken, haughty and aloof,
unlike, (I sensed), his God, and ours.

In a Parched Land

Early evening light, wide spaces
without freedom; woods bounding, gates,

playing fields with their white posts
abandoned; I was circling — a ghost —

the gravel path at the perimeter,
clothed in loneliness, without centre —

when he was there, coming against me,
tall, long-coated, straight; I could see

his cane trembling, testing before him; distinguished,
old, figure-head of our history,

near blind, a ghost, he was circling, too;
I stood aside; he stopped; "who . . .?"

"only a novice, sir," I said; and he replied
"I also, am a novice", and he smiled

into, and out of, darkness; and we moved on,
he back to his loneliness, I to mine.

Our Days are Consumed like Smoke

She had been strong; withstanding;
granny-soft in woollens; yielding;
a perfect candidate for pain.

Fullness of life and body failed her;
she seemed to offer some consent and soon
her talcumed skin was coloured

by the flush of death; waiting;
she was leaving us, settling
in the hospice for the dying, still

in touch, the old arm reaching.
Late morning, a nurse drew the curtain round,
sunshine outside, bright flowers

patterned on the cloth, the runners
scringed and left us shivering;
sealing her in, us out;

I heard the rending of metal,
steel tearing as the curtains
moved between her and God.

When the doctors left she had become
an object, shuddering, something essential
gone from her, and who is left

to love her? Truth, and all the
varieties of suffering
yielding her up, purged, to her God.

Sing to the Lord a New Song

There were words that sounded in the mouth
like a stone's fall echoing in a cavern;
introibo, we sang, *ad altare Dei* :
perfect words that sang like the bellows organ
filling the island church to bursting;
Tower of Ivory, House of Gold;

and saints we named, like Cosmas, Damian;
words whose strength was of Carrara marble
and the locked bronzed doors of Rheims cathedral;
how they skittered about in our island air
like tropical birds whipped well off course.
In the space dividing earth from heaven

things fall easily and words must be redeemed
out of the musty pockets of cassocks,
out of the waxen distance of high cupboards;
these, then, may be the new saints :
Beckett, Sam, of the stared-down void;
Mandela, saint, of our impossible hope;

Cardenal, Guttierez, Leonardo Boff,
saints of the nouveau poor of the new world;
St Mary Robinson and St John Hume;
R.S.Thomas, saint, and saint Ted Hughes;
and words again ring timely in the mouth
and God stands broken and unkempt and home.

Truth shall Spring out of the Earth:
and Justness shall Look down from Heaven

This is the noise of politics,
of propaganda, poets, of the church;
so much noise we can scarcely hear
the cries of horror . . .

They turn up on the doorstep
like forecasters of bad weather,
choose suppertime, and vulnerability;
when we pretend we are not in

they drop their noisome words
through the ear of the letterbox,
new clinics, promises, psalms,
with flattering pictures of themselves;

and when they gather, the chattering!
We deserve better from them,
needing that silence where the febrile
flower of truth may someday grow.

His Mother, and His Mother's Sister, Mary, and Mary Magdalene

They stood, and all the forces of government
were massed around them;
twilight quickened suddenly to murk; spent
with grief they were witnesses, though mute, to this

apotheosis of violence;
you cannot reach strained fists
to threaten God down to earth,
however delicate the wrists

or sensitive the bones of the feet;
this is the nadir of what has been more
than perfect, is beauty supreme in ugliness,
eternal silence in one spasmic cry of despair;

attention wholly given
and absolute presence there, were prayers
enough and over
and all the shells of the self forsaken; theirs,

too, silence before the trembling
and everything reduced to baseless trust,
that joy is sorrow and sorrow joy,
that what was absolute power must,

through such paroxysms of pain, become
love; God that was broken
is unbroken, the final yes
set up as sign and token

of contradiction; at the dead centre
nothing remains but aspiration;
what they witnessed was silence
and death and extreme humiliation

nailed forever in place
till the thoroughly broken dead can prove
their blood and rottenness, and with new grace
draw to the source of loveliness and love.

Owl

He stood, sideways to the light;
there was a black butterfly on the kitchen wall,
fluttering, beautiful, beyond possessing;

he shifted, and a predator's head
with high ears, rotated cunningly;
I watched, not knowing yet

what to ask of it, for who —
shiftless and standing sideways to the light —
has not puffed up and gestured

eye-bright, to his enlarged ego on the wall;
the world about us, we have learned,
is the making of what we yearn for,

though shifting, the way passing cars at night
send light-and-shadow shapes
across the bedroom wall.

He died, and I remembered it
as I watched him lowerd out of the light
into everlasting dark.

In his Own Image

He curls into a city doorway,
his night-home refrigerator packing-cases,
his mattress last month's newspapers;

the clattering of footsteps past him has grown less,
chocolate wrappers whip in the wind and a can
dances passionately in the gutter;

shaven-headed and unshaven, he is a gathering
of man-stench and garbage-smells,
his eyes are dried-out seeds and you look

quickly away; sometime in the night one hand
will fall heavily out along the pavement, palm
upward to the stars, fingers bent so you can see

the perfect quarter-moons of his fingernails,
the life-line like a contour-map of the sky;
unlovable, abdication, God's image,

his abhorred body is the sheen on glass
that turns the curious aside to where we stand,
immersed in self as in lambs-wool coats, certain

of our place in the world, our destination.

Icarus series of booklets by John F. Deane

No. 1 : "Far Country" (1992)

No. 2 : "For the Living and the Dead" (1994)
 (from the Swedish of Tomas Tranströmer)

No. 3 : "Upon Foreign Soil" (1999)